RESTORING

THE

AMERICAN DREAM!

From: "KEEPING AMERICA STRONG AGAIN!"

By

Dennis Andrew Ball,

author, THE BALL DOCTRINE:

"Creating Peace & Prosperity In Every Nation!"

Copyright © 2017 Dennis Andrew Ball

ISBN 13: 9781979768825
10: 197976882X

<u>DEDICATION</u>

"THIS BOOK IS DEDICATED TO AMERICANS WHO SACRIFICE EVERYDAY TO PRESERVE PROTECT & DEFEND OUR LIBERTY AND FREEDOM FOR OUR CHILDREN AND GENERATIONS TO COME! NOW THE TIME HAS COME FOR A NEW GENERATION OF AMERICANS TO TAKE THE REIGNS OF STATE & MAKE THEM WORK AS THEIR OWN IN THE BEST INTERSTS OF THE PEOPLE, THEIR CHILDREN, THEIR FAMILIES AND GENERATIONS TO COME!"

TABLE OF CONTENTS

Dedication

Acknowledgment

Authors' Foreword

———

ACKNOWLEDGMENT

To The COURAGE President George Washington Demonstrated At A Time Of Great Danger To Our Nation During Uncertain Times In American History.

Author's Foreword

I am reminded by history past the history of the United States would not be complete if it were not for those gallant men and women who in the face of danger, proceeded to do something Special about it! America's very existence is tied to her economic health which has seen a great deal of danger for THE PEOPLE since 1913 starting at Jekyl Island, Georgia by a group of elitist Domestic & International bankers with the participation of the Congress of the United States on Christmas Eve. We are living in time where our nation is divided by forces adverse to the sustainability Of the American traditional family and our children.

Since the death of President Kennedy, events in America and the World have continued to show all of us how vulnerable our economic system is to currency manipulation and deficit spending by governments and the Congress of these United States, the result being a bloated deficit with borrowing and spending unaccountable to The Citizenry & States of the United States; including fiscal policies, laws and acts contrary to The BEST INTERESTS of ALL Americans.

RESTORING THE AMERICAN DREAM addresses these abuses showing the way out of the family crisis generations of government entities have allowed to be created including every President since President Kennedy.

*Now the magic of **Real Change** can come through RESTORING THE AMERICAN DREAM! From KEEPING AMERICA STRONG AGAIN!"*

1. FORGOTTEN FAMILIES!

The *history of America* would not be complete if it were not for the men and women who sacrificed so much of themselves for a new nation and its children. Of course, much can be said of those who plotted against them and used them to profit at their expense. For those they must answer for us we must correct their mistakes for our children and generations to come. This then, becomes the back ground and back drop of *RESTORING THE AMERICAN DREAM!*

"You cannot help the poor by destroying the Rich." "You cannot keep out of trouble by spending more than you earn." "You cannot lift the wage earner by pulling down the wage payer" – Abraham Lincoln

---

"I have always been afraid of banks."

"One man with courage makes a majority"

"It is to be regretted that the rich and powerful too often bend the acts of government to their own selfish purposes." "Take time to deliberate but when the time for action arrives, stop thinking and go in." – *Andrew Jackson*

Let it be said, that America's finest hours are yet to come because the Children Of America can make a contribution to not only our Nation but also the World!

We are the product of generations past, present and future with the belief that our rights come from God; NOT THE STATE at a great cost to those who fought and died for them! That was the Social Contract created in 1781 at Yorktown-Gloucester Bay, Virginia.

The monuments laid at the reefs of those so honored are a testament to the sacrifice of so many for the hope that their sacrifice would *bear*. A proud nation was born and with it the greatest nation on earth in the history of man, *"AMERICA!"*

THE NATIONAL BACKGROUND

Early History

What was assumed by those in power was taken for granted by those struggling to live out their dreams. *AMERICA* was a land of opportunity because it's people made it their priority to continue living out their dreams for a better life for themselves and those for their children.

Colonial America grew at an astounding rate by the span of time from the founding of the Republic at Jamestown, Virginia 1607 until the last entry known as Georgia Colony 1732.

Of course, many events in between the time of founding and establishing Colonial life dominated the culture legally and politically; particularly making it possible for 2.5 million people to realize their value because the Bible was read in the home, the schools and the Supreme Court! Ethics & Morales were also taught in the home practicing honesty and good business including honest services. The attitudes within the culture was fairness as the colonies grew in population and farming. As a result, the *Great Migration* ensued so that by the beginning of the War For Independence, *AMERICA* had enough population to fight England for it. And so we did on July 4, 1776 by way of the Declaration Of Independence, Congress, Philadelphia, Pennsylvania.

Now comes RESTORING THE AMERICAN DREAM. What does it say and what does it mean?

From KEEPING AMERICA STRONG AGAIN, I have attempted to prove and provide the winning strategy to strengthen the American economic system to conform with Constitutional guarantees of *due process* ignored by every President since Kennedy!

But in a more transparent way, Restoring The American Dream means addressing both the abuses and solutions in relationships that cause concern relevant to marriage and divorce, two of the most caustic problems of our age.

Unlike generations past where the institution of marriage was sacred & supported, today's society places it as a trophy to be paraded then discarded by the players. In a mere 75 years attitudes changed that now risk a total and complete Social Collapse toward attitudes that threaten even the most committed couples.

The *forgotten family* has been discarded made to *suffer* by the callous and evil behavior of our Institutions and its leaders including Judges, Lawyers, Politicians, Legislators, Business leaders, Trade Unions and a *Shadow Government Unaccountable to no one!* The Rule Of Law has been ignored and with it the forgotten family!

2. STOP TAKING OUR JOBS!

Since the early 70's, America has continued to experience a downward cycle ever since the death of President Kennedy.

Vietnam, Arab Oil Embargo, Unions, Foreign competition all made their dent including the disaster called WATERGATE.

Government spending continued to rise even with the election of a fiscal conservative in Ronald Reagan. Debt continued to pile up while the Gross National Product declined creating a trade deficit in the $Billions$ of dollars.

This in turn gave rise to the dot com bubble with the signing of the "Free Trade" agreement known as NAFTA. Since then, every President since Bill Clinton has failed to correct a spiraling federal deficit impacting the quality of life upon the American family.

Since 9/11 American industry has lost

over 50,000 factories and counting. It is a wasteland in areas that were buzzing with distribution and manufacturing products. Some communities are engaged in making Unions accountable to their members to protect them from job loss in the event the worker's factory relocates.

But as late as May, 2011 this author was proposing to reverse this trend away from America to bring capital back to our shores by means to support the families of the United States Of America.

Which raises the question, "How Would You Do It?" Besides creating a tide that lifts all boats, the cost of production and materials compared elsewhere, becomes the economic engine that drives supporting the middle class family.

If we learn anything from the last three Presidents, it is that the means of production is vital in order to create an economic engine!

Factories just don't happen! They require an educated work base in skills necessary to do the job.

Management is responsible for creating a work environment that is both conducive to worker productivity and compensation. One without the other is insufficient and causes lack of worker productivity and apathy which leads to termination.

Failure on the part of any party engaged in this process, spells certain disaster that has come to visit our shores. Reversing this trend makes it imperative that business, labor and government get on the same page to correct the abuses in the system impacting the labor force.

Raising a family on minimum wage is impossible needing the support of a living wage requiring a restructuring of the economic system to create the incentives for Keeping America Strong Again!

Undoubtedly, that responsibility lays with the community and how they wish to approach the problem. However, ultimately The task of educating and financing job creation will require creating a work base that makes our nation productive.

Socialism be damned! Free-enterprise Capitalism on a level playing field will erase a gross trade imbalance and bring American jobs back to our shores.

Capital to do that will come from industry that has parked its profits off shore waiting to reinvest in America and her people! Trade deals that place American jobs at risk will be no more. The American worker and their family must become "Number #1" for our nation and her children.

In "KEEPING AMERICA STRONG AGAIN", I discuss what must happen to create a new economic system for America to recover from years of abuse since 1913.

3. MAKE OUR HOMES SAFE!

That model is the right one because of what President Kennedy did to limit the abuse of power by the Federal Reserve System. His Acts are still valid today!

'What the President alluded to was the pernicious attitude upon the nation by the Cartel of International Bankers President Woodrow Wilson had signed into law a day prior to Christmas Eve December 23, 1913.'

The Federal Reserve Act was a continuation of the financial abuse created upon the nation prior to its signing, in 1791 & 1816. Only Old Hickory shut down the Bank Of The United States in 1836 paying off the Federal Debt of $7,000,000.00 with The Federal Treasury. It still stands today.

Because of what the Banking Cartel had done to the nation, President Kennedy was intent in undoing. Because the Federal Reserve Bank is a Central Bank its Charter exempted it from accountable oversight to any government entity. Its powers had to be reigned in.

John Kennedy made it his business to do just that by signing E.O. 11110 effectively transferring control of the Bank out of their hands to the United States Treasury. This in turn had the chilling effect of neutralizing the Bank's Charter putting it out of business. The Gold Standard still was backing US Dollar currency for The People.

Signed June 4, 1963, the Order provided for the printing of both Silver Certificates & United States Notes exempting the words Federal Reserve Note. Both bills showed their authenticity to the United States Treasury and were circulated prior to and shortly after President Kennedy's death November 22, 1963. That Order has never been rescinded but ignored by every President since Kennedy. The National debt does not belong to the American People but to the private banking cartel known as the Federal Reserve Bank Of NY & its Branches!

****** (for educational Art display only)**

RS - ($2.00 United States Note Circa 1963)

+++++++++++++++++++++++++++++++++++

+++++++++++++RS   -   ($5.00   United

States Note Circa 1963)

****(for   educational   Art   display   only)

The moral of the story is that for people to be safe their currency must be protected from financial exploitation by any entity so inclined.

Our homes are only as safe as the economic health and wellbeing of our economic system. Most Citizens are devoid of this knowledge as are politicians or simply do not care as long as their own interests are served.

President Kennedy also spoke by his words and deeds both prior and after his death for he had put into motion policies that are still alive today recognized to keep the family safe.

The question most important that must be Answered by all of us to the extent we work for the Best Interests of our family, then who's interests are we working?. To abuse others for personal profit is a crime that must be explored in FAMILIES ARE FOREVER!

4. FAMILIES ARE FOREVER!

Not enough is said about the abuse our culture has created upon its people. Our social mentality is blighted by the sheer numbers required to survive in an ever ending spiral of social and economic decline.

.   *For* profit institutions have replaced those who once looked to families to care for the sick and the elderly. Prison overcrowding too! All with a mandate by governments both State and Federal that suck us dry and makes us weak. Enough!

Families Are Forever and must be affirmed in and by any society. Why? Because there is only one race, the human race and emulates the values that support the worth of children and their role in society.

Because they are our greatest asset, we must *not* abuse them but alternatively help them succeed where Society has failed them. That failure resides within both the economic and social institutions that have ground to a halt because of the negligent behavior coming from Washington D.C. and State Governors who have a duty to uphold the virtues of the traditional heterosexual nuclear family to make and keep it strong within their own community.

How can they do it you ask? Several ways. Principally by making their first priority restoring the economic health and vitality within their own locality.

How can Illinois be responsible for what does or does not happen in Missouri or Iowa? The movers & shakers in those communities may have some interest in mineral and water rights, but cannot be expected to change the economic and social climate of others until & unless they are able to address concerns that are their own.

To go along to get along those days are gone. We The People are faced with an economic and social crisis that mirrors in some areas during the great depression; especially within certain minorities and ethnicity groups.

"Every Man A King" in his own right makes for good publicity by people like Huey Long, former governor of Louisiana. Problem is it does not address the opposite need to work in the Family's Best Interest as a Social model for *Real Change!*

That comes when the local community decides to get to work to improving the quality of life for all; not just some! I will speak further about that in *NO CHILD LEFT BEHIND!*

Can we do better? You bet we can! Our public resolve for our children is a testament of how committed we are to doing that which must be done! Our families too! How can we work in their Best Interests and deny them the support they need to survive and thrive. That would be sacrilege upon the most vulnerable members of society.

Our hearts go out to families destroyed By neglect, indifference or sheer violence that destroys their ability to survive and thrive. Our culture has grown weary of those who prey upon it for their own profit by any means harming the very members that make it work. This is unacceptable and must be Stopped!

Violence begins in the heart so the good book extolls. "Vengeance" is mine thus sayeth the Lord! For all that it's worth, I too have trouble but dedicate myself to the virtues and ideals upon which economic and social justice rest at "HOME". There is where we get our values and our commitments to guide our lives in the direction they will go.

My prayer is for everyone reading these will come to the same conclusion I have that Families Are Forever and should be treated as such in a community of caring and educated people for their children and gen4erations to come.

Once we do the commitment, then we are on our way to bringing the change we all desire, need and require for our children and generations to come. We must educate our kids to know right from wrong and motivate them to be the best they can be. We parents, have a great responsibility to raise up a child in the path they should go and at the end they will not depart from what they were taught.

We must become educated ourselves to know the ways and wiles of the World and those close to us. The reading of my texts is a good start along with focus groups to talk about the BEST INTERESTS of the family and what that *really* means!

As before, our hearts go out to those touched by tragedy in today's society. Everyday, we read about *death* at the door of Citizens' being victimized by others from opposite ends of the social economic ladder.

I am reminded how difficult it is to correct events others create for us that bring harm into our lives. But I pray that you will find it within yourself to do that which must get done to resolve for yourself the damage that was done or being done to you and your loved ones right now! FAMILIES ARE FOREVER AND THEY REQUIRE OUR SUPPORT TO SURVIVE & THRIVE!

5.TEACH CHILDREN WELL!

The Federal Government is undisciplined by design the case for a balanced budget and with it a Balanced Budget Amendment.

The case can also be made that unfunded mandates it creates causes harm to the States by depleting their resources for the citizens in their State.

SOPHISTRY has literally changed the Mission & Purpose of Federal government to one of consumption & waste of Taxpayer dollars.

Entitlements, Earmarks, Pork, Mandates, Gerrymandering and getting re-elected with few term limits have caused a burgeoning national debt and crisis of confidence in our nation's economy.

How much more can the nation endure

until real change addresses the real problems of Income Inequality? Only time will tell, but in this author's humble opinion, it needs to start NOW!

Our children will thank us for making it and them our priority to secure their futures and those to come.

Replacing the 16th Amendment with a Balance Budget Amendment makes sense. Bridling the Federal Budget from politicians who use their position to buy votes with tax payer dollars in the form of Pork, Earmarks Mandates, Entitlements, Sophistry is wrong!

How many school lunch programs for little kids are we depriving by masking our true intentions in ways that hurt our nation and our Children?

On the streets of Washington D.C. I

witnessed in 2012 homeless people and families sleeping on the streets and sides of buildings for not enough food to eat or a place to sleep. In a country as rich as these United States, I saw what poverty does to people and the aftermath of hopelessness makes. Skilled Labor prevents that social experience of homelessness. Making life affordable is the challenge we face and it starts with the budget economy that works for all Americans and their families. From there, Citizenship becomes the responsibility of us all to see our children are educated and our community productive. Skilled labor solves a multitude of problems politicians create.

A Balanced Budget amendment will keep Federal departments from overspending and gaming the system for more resources the next fiscal year. With the States processing the tax on consumption, they will be in the position to take control of the purse to empower them to control the size and depth of the Federal government because controls on spending and borrowing do not exist. It is within their discretion based on revenues collected at the State level to fund having the effect of limiting the size of government and its wasteful spending practices on non-essential services & programs based on the taxes in their control.

But to a larger degree, the idea that the vast majority of Americans pay NO Income Tax is a testament that something is wrong with this picture that must be corrected not only for the good of society but for the good

Of the Country.

Teaching our children well teaches them respect for themselves and introduces them to a culture that values them and opinions they have regardless of how little or how big they express them.

There in lays an opportunity for mothers and fathers to show their children the value and importance of communication in their relationships at an early age in development.

I am reminded as a child in my own childhood how ignorant I was to life's important reality's and lessons about our human development and its aftermath. How mothers communicate with daughters and fathers with their sons about attitudes that drive us and make us who we become!

It is tragic that despite the number of

marriages each year the rate of divorce continues to be high amongst couples. This shows a problem exists within the culture especially compared before and after World War II.

I attribute much of it to ignorance amongst the sexes especially during puberty and adolescence. Society's expectations are so low regarding interpersonal relationships that it becomes a contributing factor in keeping divorce lawyers busy in family courts.

Human beings as complex as they are tend to gravitate toward others they agree. However, within the area of interpersonal relationships between the sexes, intimacy is a major factor that often defines and drives them. This, I believe is a major contributing factor in the breakdown and failure of them in Western Society.

Until society is ready and willing to talk openly about human sexuality amongst the sexes, divorce will remain a constant to keep divorce lawyers & family courts in business.

'If you are not working in the Best Interests Of your family, who's interests are you working fore?'

Divorce after marriage is a mistake event that should be avoided by not marrying someone who does not share your values or motivations. Communicate with others your interests and desires within an interpersonal relationship so you know what is good or bad for you personally.

Don't assume anything but communicate so you can learn and know the likes and dislikes of others that make you feel good to be with them or not with them. If we wish to see our families restored, we will have to consider doing and communicating for our benefit. If failure persists, it means that the relationship has changed requiring action to cure for the other members. However, the tragedy is that it might have been avoided if more was known prior to the marriage and subsequent children it produced.

Our kids deserve better than what society in America is producing. Let us learn and grow together to solve family abuse amongst members by becoming educated in the area of interpersonal intimacy and its power to nourish or destroy intimate relationships.

6. NO CHILD LEFT BEHIND!

"The States Have The Responsibility For Administering, Collecting & Allocating The Sales Tax To The Treasury." – The Fair Tax

Because NO provision was written into The United States Constitution regulating Borrowing or spending by the Congress of these United States, there exists and has for years, a problem regulating the National Debt beginning in 1913 continuing until now.

That problem is DEFICIT SPENDING. borrowing and paying Interest on the Debt with taxpayer dollars out of the Federal Treasury. This is what George Washington warned America at its founding and to keep America "Free" from its burden as if foreign Army's had absconded with government property without ever firing a shot!

In our history, the problem has grown to become UNACCOUNTABLE DEFICIT BORROWING & SPENDING making it IMPOSSIBLE for the Federal Government to police itself without shutting it down.;

Our history also shows that since 1913, *America* has failed to put in place safeguards to prevent this unaccountable cycle to come to an END!. WE THE PEOPLE, demand that this government stop it's endless cycle for the good of our Country, our Children and Generations to come!

The Ruling Banking Families in the Federal Reserve Central Bank know exactly the burden they have created by design upon the American people & their children. They know the bigger the debt on the nation the greater their profits from the DEFICIT. They are not about to reduce it because they know they don't have too. But that does not release them from the liability of their FRAUD on the nation. Specifically, Executive Order E.O 11110 signed June 4, 1963 by then President John Fitzgerald Kennedy transferring control of America's monetary system to the United States Treasury.

We can see that in June 1963, America Borrowed $305,859,632,996.41 backed by Gold & Silver. Today, the debt has grown and keeps growing to unacceptable limits all to make the Bankers more money on interest charged on THEIR DEBT.

-Here's The Evidence-

From 1963 to 1999 The National debt climbed from $305,000,000,000.00 billions to over $5,000,000,000,000.00 trillions.in a matter of 36 years. Now it is approaching $20,000,000,000,000,.00 with trillions in Unfunded mandates stuck to the States.

The Cartel has made its business to loan the Federal Government any amount of *fiat* currency it requires as long as it pays the interest on the debt. They have also made it their business to cause harm to Citizens by causing the government to collect taxes to pay them. The debt however, cannot be paid *but it can be forgiven.*

How? Because it is backed by nothing! The same people who formed the Cartel sold the Country that the Banks would take care of the financial needs of the nation so long as the nation paid them interest on the debt. The Federal Reserve System is neither Federal nor a Reserve of Currency nor a System. It is in effect a Banker's Cartel who lends *fiat currency with no value for interest payments to the members of the Cartel every month administered by the IRS & Treasury.*

This relationship was designed by the Scientists of the Federal Reserve System. They knew exactly what they should do to make the "System" work for them opposite the American Taxpayer.

In effect, it is a corrupt institution that Funds the International Monetary Fund & The World Bank.

There is absolutely no evidence that Executive Order 11110 signed June 4, 1963 has been rescinded or the wording that nullified it despite other President's issues.

We are left that since every President since Lyndon Johnson, has ignored it that perhaps fearful that if they were to follow its directive, they too might be killed. Both Lincoln and Kennedy believed the *Nation* should issue and regulate its own currency; not a foreign bank masquerading around as a Federal entity but a private banking cartel.

The nation had seen this before during the presidency of Andrew Jackson (1829-1837).

THE BANK OF THE UNITED STATES was shut down by Jackson but an attempt was made on his life. Jackson, founder of the Democratic Party surmised as warned by George Washington that the currency of the nation was sovereign to the United States Treasury and should stay in its control both in the manufacturing and minting of printed and coined currency.

The inflation non-backed currency wars on the dollar devaluing the dollars' worth in terms of purchasing power and payment of debt release. Diluting the economy with unbacked green backs is a recipe for more inflation and higher prices.

Backed securities with Gold or Silver makes for a much more stable economy disallowing the government from over spending and causing families harm by a reckless and selfish policy of greed.

Our children are at risk to the Federal government to economically fail because they will become 'slaves to the state" no longer able to control a rogue policy of self enrichment at the expense of the taxpayers and their families. The Federal government will have to learn to live within its means like Citizens must live within a budget. The Charter Bank will replace the Central Bank aka Federal Reserve System.

The boom and bust cycles in the *history* of the nation is over. Economic prosperity for America will be measured in real dollars backed by Gold or Silver instead of nothing!

The national debt will be gone and the dawning of a new era in funding will begin! War bonds, Saving Bonds, Treasury Bills all have their place raising money for worthy Causes and Investments for the The People!

The IRS, 16th Amendment, Federal Reserve Act, Income Tax should all go away

Leading to the introduction of a Fair Tax on Consumption or spending. Because half of America pays income tax, it is not fair to tax Income on those who do pay. A Fair Tax will mandate that everybody pays tax on what they spend. That is fair & equitable.

No income tax means individuals and families can keep more of their hard earned money for themselves to support their lives and their property, It also means they that control the purse controls the size of the government Local, State and Federal..

The Fair Tax does that at the point of sale incorporating a tax on goods & services equitably distributed for the benefit of the taxpayers. The effect is that reduced revenues means smaller government for our benefit and our families. This stops the burgeoning tax burden and creates a system fair to WE THE PEOPLE!

Now industry can return to America because tax on income has been removed opening the market to financial prosperity for all.

Industry will find its way back building the factories employing the people creating economic prosperity and accountability for our children and generations to come. In effect, "NO CHILD LEFT BEHIND!"

7. ABOLISH PROBATE COURTS!

America's destiny demands her people do for her children that which requires their economic, emotional security, benefit and welfare for now and generations to come.

To do that means being educated in the misconduct of this government creating a new model by which its Citizens function.

Unlike the Federal Reserve System, A Fair Tax does not require an Amendment to the Constitution to make it work. It is suggested and recommended for a Balance Budget Amendment replace it to keep the government's budget in check with its income.

Since 1913, the Federal government is dependent on tax and spend policies that cause harm to our children and families.

Inflation on prices of goods and services can be directly attributed to the number of non-backed currency dollars floating from the Federal Reserve Bank. Whether its an entry on their computers, the debt continues to grow which the cartel wants to realize the income on interest that debt generates to it.

Why this is allowed to continue should be of great concern to The People of the United States. Until this is changed and a new model appears, *America* will continue to be held hostage to the bankers and their *cartel* families.

In addition, the *National Debt* as a Product of the Gross National Product (GDP) is comprised of Public, Foreign Countries, and Americans. But the Federal Reserve Banks lend to the Federal government and that debt should go away. That would reduce the National Debt by 70% with the reset owed to trusts and countries.

That would greatly reduce the stress created on the taxpayers to support the debt. In effect it would relieve the burden on the people to keep more of their hard earned dollars in their pockets thereby increasing their ability to save and build an equity for themselves and their families.

___PROBATE ABUSE IN STATE COURTS!___

Now, that all said, my greatest concern is that your money and property will go away from you and your family by those in the Judiciary of State Probate Courts.

In my first book "AMERICA 2000:

"Foundations For Generations! I speak of the economic abuse done to innocent family members by State Sponsored Guardianship proceedings that abscond with ALL OUR MONEY & PROPERTY.

These proceedings are conducted by Probate Courts on the County level with the State Bar, Supreme Court & Legislature participating. It amounts to a whole sale scam of that person's property and assets into the pockets of third parties who had nothing to do to earn it or interest in protecting it. In other words, Probate Courts are nothing less than agents of SWINDLE upon the families of America.

Some have compared them to Courts of Human Trafficking & a new form of slavery they once were used during that period in

American history. Human ownership by Proxy by State Governments has returned to our shores by a hell bent Judiciary to suck every penny out of the family and make sure it is accomplished before they die!

The practice is so wide spread, families plundered, pilfered and thrust into poverty within a short period of time from the initial proceedings. It is a threat to every American who has accumulated any assets & property over their lifetime.

These tyrannical proceedings are destroying the Republic as it was intended allowing criminal elements to profit at the expense of THE PEOPLE!

It is also occurring in the Family Courts. Children held for ransom being kidnapped and placed in another system of corruption where money from Title IV funding has destroyed the sanctity of the home and made children chattel to be controlled and used for State profit. This was instituted during the Clinton administration by Hillary & Bill Clinton, setting a very bad precedent for our nation & future for our Children & families.

8. REMOVE FAMILY COURTS!

Title IV-D Social Security Act

As if Probate Courts weren't enough to cause us harm, the Clinton's made sure that children and their parents would be a Bonanza for State governments to profit & destroy.

Title 42-D of the Social Security Act is lengthy as it is cumbersome by design. Lawmakers purposely create titles and sections to cause confusion in the administration of the Act. It is design to reward those making decisions for parents and children who have not their Best Interests and are only doing it for money paid them at the State level by the Federal government entitlement programs.

The Clintons' knew the damage this would do the nation's children by separating them from their parents. It also allowed Big-Pharma ample opportunity to profit manufacturing neuro-inhibitors to mess with their brains at a young age. This is criminal making it probable that the laws must be repealed and amended out of the language.

My concern is that children have a good Childhood free from the shenanigans of the State Courts using laws that do harm to families and their children.

Society requires strong families to survive and thrive; not the watered down milk toast the State has to dish out by making money off them!

This is the way of the World, its legal system, attorneys, courts and judges. Hillary Clinton is an attorney; so was Bill Clinton. Both of them did tremendous damage to the family unit that is currently in repair by the likes of those individuals who identify the problems and are engaged in doing and changing the outcome.

The Young & The Old are targeted as Profit centers for the State. This must Change. Our Society has gone secular in its attitudes toward parents and children and justify their intentions in the "Best Interests of the Child." Yet children go without and suffer at the hands of adults removed from their lives and not part of their parents lives. This is not in the Family's Best Interests!

9. AN AMORAL SOCIETY!

As though time and distance could be seen into a looking glass what is to come, history shows us what has happened to nations when the laws of economic$ are violated by those in authority.

No doubt, the nations of the World still have much to learn from the mistakes of previous generations culminating in their demise. The graph below illustrates nations' who in fact make those mistakes.

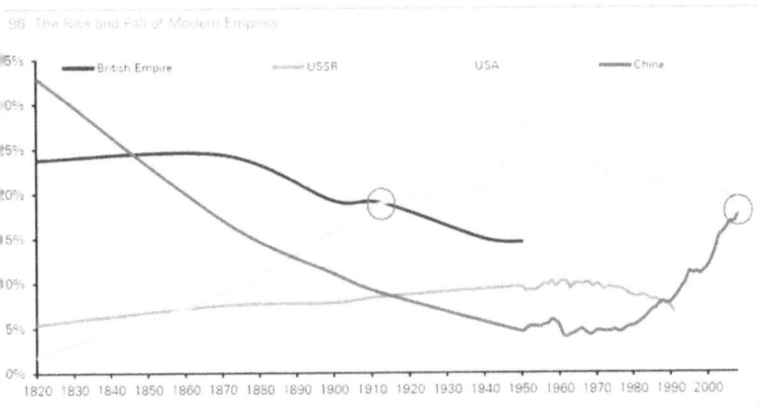

It would appear to this author that for years the economic policies that created mass chaos within market conditions are based on the notion that profits trump the BEST INTERESTS of people, particularly those with the ability to exploit others for personal gain.

THE BALL DOCTRINE points out the absolute need to *reign-in* the money powers that have created so much harm to so many people throughout World History. This was President Kennedy's vision:

'He believed the family *reigned supreme* as the basic social unit of every nation'.

Speech after speech, the affirmations of America's global supremacy over those nation's who created harm to the national security of the United States and its foreign policy directives were met head on by the Kennedy administration. Kennedy was a man of *destiny* and his policies created serious challenges for the establishment.

To that end, I have attempted to show what is lacking in the economic health of the nation. Central banks cause harm in the modern world because their policies are corrupted from within by policies created in 1910 and beyond starting at *Jekyl Island, Georgia.*

What is needed now is an act that corrects and cancels the harm that began over 100 years ago.

'THE BALL ACT' makes it possible. Conceived in *Liberty*, the act affirms the treason of Woodrow Wilson signing the

Federal Reserve Act on December 23, 1913 while Congress was out of session during Christmas.

A progressive, he violated his Oath of Office as President allowing enemies of The People to exploit the Constitution! As long as Central Banks could charge the federal government interest on non-backed money, the corrupt establishment allowed it to pass. President Kennedy knew the Constitutional Powers of Separation of the three branches of government and that in effect it was the United States Treasury should be in control of America's *monetary and currency policy.*

This violation of America's sovereignty showed Kennedy what previous Presidents also knew: 'The issuing of money was to come through Congress; not a Central Bank!

In other words, the nation's business was to stay with the nation; affirmed by previous generations and their administrations. Third party Central Banks is what Andrew Jackson shut down The Bank Of The United States during his presidency in 1833 & paid off the national debt with funds from the federal treasury backed by gold and silver bullion.

The founders had warned the nation that monetary policy could be circumvented; the nation threatened by policy violating the sovereignty of the United States causing the loss of all that had been fought and died.

With the signing of Executive Order 11110, President Kennedy effectively shut down the Federal Reserve System and they were alarmed; especially the families who benefit & support it. America's sovereignty was reaffirmed and the national debt was in check. The nation was on its way to policies that would lead to greatness amongst the World's nations affirming free-enterprise Capitalism superior to Marxist-Socialist Communism in the struggle of ideas for World dominance.

The result of this act will be to return American sovereignty back to itself with a new tax system eliminating the need for its Citizens to pay interest on debt. A balance budget insures the government stays within its means to pay for what it spends. Gold & Silver returns to back government issued Tender regulated by the States as to moneys Collected from the Fair Tax on spending.

Other debt to Trust funds & Foreign Countries paid back to refund our debt.

10. STAYING STRONG!

With the advent that *positive* change makes on the nation and the world, The People will be vilified. Years of abuse by an intrusive and corrupt system of swindle and scandal will finally be gone never to return.

The Federal Reserve System has its Tentacles in the International Monetary Fund (IMF) and the World Bank (WB).

Every nation is vulnerable to the Central Bank policy of *fiat capital* like Problems it creates in Greece & Venezuela.

The Bankers have created a fail proof System of banking that works for them at expense of their depositors. By weakening the dollar through dumping dollars into the market, prices rise because it takes more of it to pay for essential goods and services in relationship to the nation's Gross National Product (GNP). President Kennedy was all over it and knew that it could bankrupt the country; something he wanted to prevent!

I believe Robert Kennedy had he become President would have continued the policies his older brother created.

Both Kennedy brothers knew that War & Money corrupt a country. Both were against the exploitation of both. That is what the bankers wanted tied to The Federal Reserve System. From it, it can be conjectured that David Rockefeller and his Tri-lateral Commission & Council of Foreign Relations have directly benefited from the power the bankers have created by this debt creating system of *fiat capital.*

APPENDIX

Historical Debt Outstanding - Annual 1790 - 1849

The first fiscal year for the U.S. Government started Jan. 1, 1789. Congress changed the beginning of the fiscal year from Jan. 1 to Jul. 1 in 1842, and finally from Jul. 1 to Oct. 1 in 1977 where it remains today.

Date	Dollar Amount
07/01/1849	63,061,858.69
07/01/1848	47,044,862.23
07/01/1847	38,826,534.77
07/01/1846	15,550,202.97
07/01/1845	15,925,303.01
07/01/1844	23,461,652.50
07/01/1843	32,742,922.00
01/01/1843	20,201,226.27
01/01/1842	13,594,480.73
01/01/1841	5,250,875.54
01/01/1840	3,573,343.82
01/01/1839	10,434,221.14
01/01/1838	3,308,124.07
01/01/1837	336,957.83
01/01/1836	37,513.05

01/01/1835	33,733.05
01/01/1834	4,760,082.08
01/01/1833	7,001,698.83
01/01/1832	24,322,235.18
01/01/1831	39,123,191.68
01/01/1830	48,565,406.50
01/01/1829	58,421,413.67
01/01/1828	67,475,043.87
01/01/1827	73,987,357.20
01/01/1826	81,054,059.99
01/01/1825	83,788,432.71
01/01/1824	90,269,777.77
01/01/1823	90,875,877.28
01/01/1822	93,546,676.98
01/01/1821	89,987,427.66
01/01/1820	91,015,566.15
01/01/1819	95,529,648.28
01/01/1818	103,466,633.83
01/01/1817	123,491,965.16
01/01/1816	127,334,933.74
01/01/1815	99,833,660.15
01/01/1814	81,487,846.24
01/01/1813	55,962,827.57
01/01/1812	45,209,737.90

01/01/1811	48,005,587.76
01/01/1810	53,173,217.52
01/01/1809	57,023,192.09
01/01/1808	65,196,317.97
01/01/1807	69,218,398.64
01/01/1806	75,723,270.66
01/01/1805	82,312,150.50
01/01/1804	86,427,120.88
01/01/1803	77,054,686.40
01/01/1802	80,712,632.25
01/01/1801	83,038,050.80
01/01/1800	82,976,294.35
01/01/1799	78,408,669.77
01/01/1798	79,228,529.12
01/01/1797	82,064,479.33
01/01/1796	83,762,172.07
01/01/1795	80,747,587.39
01/01/1794	78,427,404.77
01/01/1793	80,358,634.04
01/01/1792	77,227,924.66
01/01/1791	75,463,476.52
01/01/1790	71,060,508.50

President Kennedy, The Fed And Executive Order 11110

From APFN

By Cedric X

11-20-3

Executive Order 1110 gave the US the ability to create its own money backed by silver. ...

http://www.john-f-kennedy.net/executiveorder11110.htm

On June 4, 1963, a little known attempt was made to strip the Federal Reserve Bank of its power to loan money to the government at interest. On that day President John F. Kennedy signed Executive Order No. 11110 that returned to the U.S. government the power to issue currency, without going through the Federal Reserve. Mr. Kennedy's order gave the Treasury the power "to issue silver certificates against any silver bullion, silver, or standard silver dollars in the Treasury." This meant that for every ounce of silver in the U.S. Treasury's vault, the government could introduce new money into circulation. In all, Kennedy brought nearly $4.3 billion in U.S. notes into circulation. The ramifications of this bill are enormous.

With the stroke of a pen, Mr. Kennedy was on his way to putting the Federal Reserve Bank of New York out of business. If enough of these silver certificates were to come into circulation they would have eliminated the demand for Federal Reserve notes. This is because the silver certificates are backed by silver and the Federal Reserve notes are not backed by anything. Executive Order 11110 could have prevented the national debt from reaching its current level, because it would have given the government the ability to repay its debt without going to the Federal Reserve and being charged interest in order to create the new money. Executive Order 11110 gave the U.S. the ability to create its own money backed by silver.

After Mr. Kennedy was assassinated just five months later, no more silver certificates were issued. The Final Call has learned that the Executive Order was never repealed by any U.S. President through an Executive Order and is still valid. Why then has no president utilized it? Virtually all of the nearly $6 trillion in debt has been created since 1963, and if a U.S. president had utilized Executive Order 11110 the debt would be nowhere near the current level. Perhaps the assassination of JFK was a warning to future presidents who would think to eliminate the U.S. debt by eliminating the Federal Reserve's control over the creation of money. Mr. Kennedy challenged the government of money by challenging the two most successful vehicles that have ever been used to drive up debt - war and the creation of money by a privately-owned central bank. His efforts to have all troops out of Vietnam by 1965 and Executive Order 11110 would have severely cut into the profits and control of the New York banking establishment. As America's debt reaches unbearable levels and a conflict emerges in Bosnia that will further increase America's debt, one is force to ask, will President Clinton have the courage to consider utilizing Executive Order 11110 and, if so, is he willing to pay the ultimate price for doing so?

Executive Order 11110 AMENDMENT OF EXECUTIVE ORDER NO. 10289

AS AMENDED, RELATING TO THE PERFORMANCE OF CERTAIN FUNCTIONS AFFECTING THE DEPARTMENT OF THE TREASURY

By virtue of the authority vested in me by section 301 of title 3 of the United States Code, it is ordered as follows:

Section 1. Executive Order No. 10289 of September 19, 1951, as amended, is hereby further amended-

By adding at the end of paragraph 1 thereof the following subparagraph (j):

(j) The authority vested in the President by paragraph (b) of section 43 of the Act of May 12,1933, as amended (31 U.S.C.821(b)), to issue silver certificates against any silver bullion, silver, or standard silver dollars in the Treasury not then held for redemption of any outstanding silver certificates, to prescribe the denomination of such silver certificates, and to coin standard silver dollars and subsidiary silver currency for their redemption

and --

By revoking subparagraphs (b) and (c) of paragraph 2 thereof.

Sec. 2. The amendments made by this Order shall not affect any act done, or any right accruing or accrued or any suit or proceeding had or commenced in any civil or criminal cause prior to the date of this Order but all such liabilities shall continue and may be enforced as if said amendments had not been made.

John F. Kennedy The White House, June 4, 1963.

Of course, the fact that both JFK and Lincoln met the
the same end is a mere coincidence.

Abraham Lincoln's Monetary Policy, 1865 (Page 91
of Senate document 23.)

Money is the creature of law and the creation of the
original issue of money should be maintained as the
exclusive monopoly of national Government.

Money possesses no value to the State other than that
given to it by circulation.

Capital has its proper place and is entitled to every
protection. The wages of men should be recognized
in the structure of and in the social order as more
important than the wages of money.

No duty is more imperative for the Government than
the duty it owes the People to furnish them with a
sound and uniform currency, and of regulating the
circulation of the medium of exchange so that labor
will be protected from a vicious currency, and
commerce will be facilitated by cheap and safe
exchanges.

The available supply of Gold and Silver being wholly inadequate to permit the issuance of coins of intrinsic value or paper currency convertible into coin in the volume required to serve the needs of the People, some other basis for the issue of currency must be developed, and some means other than that of convertibility into coin must be developed to prevent undue fluctuation in the value of paper currency or any other substitute for money of intrinsic value that may come into use.

The monetary needs of increasing numbers of People advancing towards higher standards of living can and should be met by the Government. Such needs can be served by the issue of National Currency and Credit through the operation of a National Banking system .The circulation of a medium of exchange issued and backed by the Government can be properly regulated and redundancy of issue avoided by withdrawing from circulation such amounts as may be necessary by Taxation, Redeposit, and otherwise. Government has the power to regulate the currency and credit of the Nation.

Government should stand behind its currency and credit and the Bank deposits of the Nation. No individual should suffer a loss of money through depreciation or inflated currency or Bank bankruptcy.

Government possessing the power to create and issue currency and creditas money and enjoying the right to withdraw both currency and credit from circulation by Taxation and otherwise need not and should not borrow capital at interest as a means of financing Governmental work and public enterprise. The Government should create, issue, and circulate all the currency and credit needed to satisfy the spending power of the Government and the buying power of the consumers. The privilege of creating and issuing money is not only the supreme prerogative of Government, but it is the Governments greatest creative opportunity.

By the adoption of these principles the long felt want for a uniform medium will be satisfied. The taxpayers will be saved immense sums of interest, discounts, and exchanges. The financing of all public enterprise, the maintenance of stable Government and ordered progress, and the conduct of the Treasury will become matters of practical administration. The people can and will be furnished with a currency as safe as their own Government. Money will cease to be master and become the servant of humanity. Democracy will rise superior to the money power.

Some information on the Federal Reserve The Federal Reserve, a Private Corporation One of the most common concerns among people who engage in any effort to reduce their taxes is, "Will keeping my money hurt the government's ability to pay it's bills?"

As explained in the first article in this series, the modern withholding tax does not, and wasn't designed to, pay for government services. What it does do, is pay for the privately-owned Federal Reserve System.

Black's Law Dictionary defines the "Federal Reserve System" as, "Network of twelve central banks to which most national banks belong and to which state chartered banks may belong. Membership rules require investment of stock and minimum reserves."

Privately-owned banks own the stock of the Fed. This was explained in more detail in the case of Lewis v. United States, Federal Reporter, 2nd Series, Vol. 680, Pages 1239, 1241 (1982), where the court said:

Each Federal Reserve Bank is a separate corporation owned by commercial banks in its region. The stock-holding commercial banks elect two thirds of each Bank's nine member board of directors.

Similarly, the Federal Reserve Banks, though heavily regulated, are locally controlled by their member banks. Taking another look at Black's Law Dictionary, we find that these privately owned banks actually issue money:

Federal Reserve Act. Law which created Federal Reserve banks which act as agents in maintaining money reserves, issuing money in the form of bank notes, lending money to banks, and supervising banks. Administered by Federal Reserve Board (q.v.).

The FED banks, which are privately owned, actually issue, that is, create, the money we use. In 1964 the House Committee on Banking and Currency, Subcommittee on Domestic Finance, at the second session of the 88th Congress, put out a study entitled Money Facts which contains a good description of what the FED is:

The Federal Reserve is a total money-making machine. It can issue money or checks. And it never has a problem of making its checks good because it can obtain the $5 and $10 bills necessary to cover its check simply by asking the Treasury Department's Bureau of Engraving to print them.

As we all know, anyone who has a lot of money has a lot of power. Now imagine a group of people who have the power to create money. Imagine the power these people would have. This is what the Fed is.

No man did more to expose the power of the Fed than Louis T. McFadden, who was the Chairman of the House Banking Committee back in the 1930s. Constantly pointing out that monetary issues shouldn't be partisan, he criticized both the Herbert Hoover and Franklin Roosevelt administrations. In describing the Fed, he remarked in the Congressional Record, House pages 1295 and 1296 on June 10, 1932, that:

Mr. Chairman, we have in this country one of the most corrupt institutions the world has ever known. I refer to the Federal Reserve Board and the Federal reserve banks. The Federal Reserve Board, a Government Board, has cheated the Government of the United States and he people of the United States out of enough money to pay the national debt. The depredations and the iniquities of the Federal Reserve Board and the Federal reserve banks acting together have cost this country enough money to pay the national debt several times over. This evil institution has impoverished and ruined the people of the United States; has bankrupted itself, and has practically bankrupted our Government. It has done this through the maladministration of that law by which the Federal Reserve Board, and through the corrupt practices of the moneyed vultures who control it.

Some people think the Federal reserve banks are United States Government institutions. They are not Government institutions. They are private credit monopolies which prey upon the people of the United States for the benefit of themselves and their foreign customers; foreign and domestic speculators and swindlers; and rich and predatory money lenders. In that dark crew of financial pirates there are those who would cut a man's throat to get a dollar out of his pocket; there are those who send money into States to buy votes to control our legislation; and there are those who maintain an international propaganda for the purpose of deceiving us and of wheedling us into the granting of new concessions which will permit them to cover up their past misdeeds and set again in motion their gigantic train of crime. Those 12 private credit monopolies were deceitfully and disloyally foisted upon this country by bankers who came here from Europe and who repaid us for our hospitality by undermining our American institutions.

The Fed basically works like this: The government granted its power to create money to the Fed banks. They create money, then loan it back to the government charging interest. The government levies income taxes to pay the interest on the debt. On this point, it's interesting to note that the Federal Reserve act and the sixteenth amendment, which gave congress the power to collect income taxes, were both passed in 1913. The incredible power of the Fed over the economy is universally admitted. Some people, especially in the banking and academic communities, even support it. On the other hand, there are those, both in the past and in the present, that speak out against it. One of these men was

President John F. Kennedy. His efforts were detailed in Jim Marrs' 1990 book, Crossfire:

Another overlooked aspect of Kennedy's attempt to reform American society involves money. Kennedy apparently reasoned that by returning to the constitution, which states that only Congress shall coin and regulate money, the soaring national debt could be reduced by not paying interest to the bankers of the Federal Reserve System, who print paper money then loan it to the government at interest. He moved in this area on June 4, 1963, by signing Executive Order 11,110 which called for the issuance of $4,292,893,815 in United States Notes through the U.S. Treasury rather than the traditional Federal Reserve System. That same day, Kennedy signed a bill changing the backing of one and two dollar bills from silver to gold, adding strength to the weakened U.S. currency.

Kennedy's comptroller of the currency, James J. Saxon, had been at odds with the powerful Federal Reserve Board for some time, encouraging broader investment and lending powers for banks that were not part of the Federal Reserve system. Saxon also had decided that non-Reserve banks could underwrite state and local general obligation bonds, again weakening the dominant Federal Reserve banks.

A number of "Kennedy bills" were indeed issued - the author has a five dollar bill in his possession with the heading "United States Note" - but were quickly withdrawn after Kennedy's death. According to information from the Library of the Comptroller of the Currency, Executive Order 11,110 remains in effect today, although successive administrations beginning with that of President Lyndon Johnson apparently have simply ignored it and instead returned to the practice of paying interest on Federal Reserve notes. Today we continue to use Federal Reserve Notes, and the deficit is at an all-time high.

The point being made is that the IRS taxes you pay aren't used for government services. It won't hurt you, or the nation, to legally reduce or eliminate your tax liability.

From The Final Call, Vol15, No.6, on January 17, 1996 (USA)

<http://www.apfn.org/apfn/eo11110.pdf>http://www.apfn.org/apfn/eo11110.pdf

http://disc.server.com/discussion.cgi?disc=149495;article=46736;title=APFN

JFK vs. Federal Reserve

On June 4, 1963, a virtually unknown Presidential decree, Executive Order 11110, was signed by President John Fitzgerald Kennedy with the intention to strip the Federal Reserve Bank of its power to loan money to the United States Federal Government at interest. With the stroke of a pen, President Kennedy declared that the privately owned Federal Reserve Bank would soon be out of business. This matter has been exhaustively researched by the Christian Common Law Institute through the Federal Register and Library of Congress, and the Institute has conclude that President Kennedy's Executive Order has never been repealed, amended, or superceded by any subsequent Executive Order. In simple terms, it is still valid.

When John Fitzgerald Kennedy, author of Profiles in Courage, signed this Order, it returned to the federal government, specifically to the Treasury Department, the Constitutional power to create and issue currency -- money -- without going through the privately owned Federal Reserve Bank. President Kennedy's Executive Order 11110 gave the Treasury Department the explicit authority: "to issue silver certificates against any silver bullion, silver, or standard silver dollars in the Treasury" [the full text is displayed below]. This means that for every ounce of silver in the U.S. Treasury's vault, the government could introduce new money into circulation based on the silver bullion physically held therein. As a result, more than $4 billion in United States Notes were brought into circulation in $2 and $5 denominations.

Although $10 and $20 United States Notes were never circulated, they were being printed by the Treasury Department when Kennedy was assassinated.

Certainly it's obvious that President Kennedy knew that the Federal Reserve Notes being circulated as "legal currency" were contrary to the Constitution of the United States, which calls for issuance of "United States Notes" as interest-free and debt-free currency backed by silver reserves in the U.S. Treasury. Comparing a "Federal Reserve Note" issued from the private central bank of the United States (i.e., the Federal Reserve Bank a/k/a Federal Reserve System), with a "United States Note" from the U.S. Treasury (as issued by President Kennedy's Executive Order), the two almost look alike, except one says "Federal Reserve Note" on the top while the other says "United States Note". In addition, the Federal Reserve Note has a green seal and serial number while the United States Note has a red seal and serial number. Following President Kennedy's assassination on November 22, 1963, the United States Notes he had issued were immediately taken out of circulation, and Federal Reserve Notes continued to serve as the "legal currency" of the nation.

Kennedy knew that if the silver-backed United States Notes were widely circulated, they would eliminated the demand for Federal Reserve Notes. This is a simple matter of economics. USNs were backed by silver and FRNs were (still are) backed by nothing of intrinsic value. As a result of Executive Order 11110, the national debt would have prevented from reaching its current level (almost all of the $9 trillion in federal debt has been created since 1963). Executive Order 11110 also granted the U.S. Government the power to repay past debt without further borrowing from the privately owned Federal Reserve which charged both principle and interest and all new "money" it "created." Finally, Executive Order 11110 gave the U.S.A. the ability to create its own money backed by silver, again giving money real value.

Perhaps President Kennedy's assassination was a warning to future presidents not to interfere with the private Federal Reserve's control over the creation of money. For, with true courage, JFK had boldly challenged the two most successful vehicles that have ever been used to drive up debt: 1) war (i.e., the Vietnam war); and, 2) the creation of money by a privately owned central bank. His efforts to have all U.S. troops out of Vietnam by 1965 combined with Executive Order 11110 would have destroyed the profits and control of the private Federal Reserve Bank.

Executive Order 11110, the AMENDMENT of EXECUTIVE ORDER No. 10289, as amended RELATING to the PERFORMANCE of CERTAIN

FUNCTIONS AFFECTING the DEPARTMENT of the TREASURY:

By virtue of the authority vested in me by section 301 of Title 3 of the United States Code, it is ordered as follows:

SECTION 1. Executive Order No. 10289 of September 19, 1951, as amended, is hereby further amended (a) By adding at the end of paragraph 1 thereof the following subparagraph (j): "(j) The authority vested in the President by paragraph (b) of section 43 of the Act of May 12, 1933, as amended (31 U.S.C. 821 (b)), to issue silver certificates against any silver bullion, silver, or standard silver dollars in the Treasury not then held for redemption of any outstanding silver certificates, to prescribe the denominations of such silver certificates, and to coin standard silver dollars and subsidiary silver currency for their redemption," and (b) By revoking subparagraphs (b) and (c) of paragraph 2 thereof.

SECTION 2. The amendment made by this Order shall not affect any act done, or any right accruing or accrued or any suit or proceeding had or commenced in any civil or criminal cause prior to the date of this Order but all such liabilities shall continue and may be enforced as if said amendments had not been made.

JOHN F. KENNEDY

THE WHITE HOUSE,

June 4, 1963

As said, Executive Order 11110 is still valid.
According to Title 3, United States Code, Section
301 dated January 26, 1998: Executive Order (EO)
10289 dated Sept. 17, 1951, 16 F.R. 9499, was as
amended by:

EO 10583, dated December 18, 1954, 19 F.R. 8725;

EO 10882 dated July 18, 1960, 25 F.R. 6869;

EO 11110 dated June 4, 1963, 28 F.R. 5605;

EO 11825 dated December 31, 1974, 40 F.R. 1003;

EO 12608 dated September 9, 1987, 52 F.R. 34617

The 1974 and 1987 amendments, added after
Kennedy's 1963 amendment, did not change or alter
any part of Kennedy's EO 11110. A search of
Clinton's 1998 and 1999 EO's and Presidential
Directives has shown no reference to any alterations,
suspensions, or changes to EO 11110.

The Federal Reserve Bank, a.k.a Federal Reserve
System, is a Private Corporation. Black's Law
Dictionary defines the "Federal Reserve System" as:

"Network of twelve central banks to which most national banks belong and to which state chartered banks may belong. Membership rules require investment of stock and minimum reserves." privately owned banks own the stock of the FED. This was explained in more detail in the case of Lewis v. United States, Federal Reporter, 2nd Series, Vol. 680, Pages 1239, 1241 (1982), where the court said: "Each Federal Reserve Bank is a separate corporation owned by commercial banks in its region. The stockholding commercial banks elect two-thirds of each Bank's nine member board of directors." In short, Federal Reserve Banks are locally controlled by their member banks.

Also, according to Black's Law Dictionary, these privately owned banks are "allowed" to issue money: "The Federal Reserve Act, created Federal Reserve banks which act as agents in maintaining money reserves, issuing money in the form of bank notes, lending money to banks, and supervising banks as administered by Federal Reserve Board (q.v.)." Thus the privately owned Federal Reserve (FED) banks are allowed to actually issue (create) the "money" we use.

In 1964, the House Committee on Banking and Currency, Subcommittee on Domestic Finance, at the second session of the 88th Congress, put out a study entitled Money Facts which contains a good description of what the FED is: "The Federal Reserve is a total moneymaking machine. It can issue money or checks. And it never has a problem of making its checks good because it can obtain the $5 and $10 bills necessary to cover its check simply by asking the Treasury Department's Bureau of Engraving to print them." Any one person or any closely knit group that has a lot of money has a lot of power. Imagine a group of people with the power to create money. Imagine the power these people would have. This is exactly what the privately owned FED is!

No man did more to expose the power of the FED than Louis T. McFadden, who was the Chairman of the House Banking Committee back in the 1930s. In describing the FED, he remarked in the Congressional Record, House pages 1295 and 1296 on June 10, 1932:

Mr. Chairman, we have in this country one of the most corrupt institutions the world has ever known. I refer to the Federal Reserve Board and the Federal reserve banks. The Federal Reserve Board, a Government Board, has cheated the Government of the United States and he people of the United States out of enough money to pay the national debt. The depredations and the iniquities of the Federal Reserve Board and the Federal reserve banks acting together have cost this country enough money to pay the national debt several times over. This evil institution has impoverished and ruined the people of the United States; has bankrupted itself, and has practically bankrupted our Government. It has done this through the maladministration of that law by which the Federal Reserve Board, and through the corrupt practices of the moneyed vultures who control it.

Some people think the Federal Reserve Banks are United States Government institutions. They are not Government institutions, departments, or agencies. They are private credit monopolies, which prey upon the people of the United States for the benefit of themselves and their foreign customers. Those 12 private credit monopolies were deceitfully placed upon this country by bankers who came here from Europe and who repaid us for our hospitality by undermining our American institutions.

The FED basically works like this: The government granted its power to create money to the FED banks. They create money, then loan it back to the government charging interest. The government levies income taxes to pay the interest on the debt. On this point, it's interesting to note that the Federal Reserve Act and the sixteenth amendment, which gave congress the power to collect income taxes, were both passed in 1913. The incredible power of the FED over the economy is universally admitted. Some people, especially in the banking and academic communities, support it. On the other hand, there are those like President John F. Kennedy, that have spoken out against it. His efforts were lauded about in Jim Marrs' 1990 book Crossfire:

Another overlooked aspect of Kennedy's attempt to reform American society involves money. Kennedy apparently reasoned that by returning to the constitution, which states that only Congress shall coin and regulate money, the soaring national debt could be reduced by not paying interest to the bankers of the Federal Reserve System, who print paper money then loan it to the government at interest. He moved in this area on June 4, 1963, by signing Executive Order 11110 which called for the issuance of $4,292,893,815 in United States Notes through the U.S. Treasury rather than the traditional Federal Reserve System. That same day, Kennedy signed a bill changing the backing of one and two dollar bills from silver to gold, adding strength to the weakened U.S. currency.

Kennedy's comptroller of the currency, James J. Saxon, had been at odds with the powerful Federal Reserve Board for some time, encouraging broader investment and lending powers for banks that were not part of the Federal Reserve system. Saxon also had decided that non-Reserve banks could underwrite general obligation bonds, again weakening the dominant Federal Reserve banks."

In a speech made to Columbia University on Nov. 12, 1963, ten days before his assassination, President John Fitzgerald Kennedy said: "The high office of the

President has been used to foment a plot to destroy the American's freedom and before I leave office, I must inform the citizen of this plight." In this matter, John Fitzgerald Kennedy appears to be the subject of his own book... a true Profile of Courage. According to the Constitution of the United States, (Article 1 Section 8), only Congress has the authority to coin Money, regulate the Value thereof, and of foreign Coin, and fix the Standard of Weights and Measures. However, since 1913 this Article has been ignored by creation and existence of the Federal Reserve Act, which has given a private owned corporation the power and authority to "create" and coin the money of United States. The Federal Reserve is comprised of 12 private credit monopolies who have been given the authority to control the supply of the "Federal Reserve Notes," interest rates and all the other monetary and banking phenomena.

The way the Federal Reserve works is this: 12 private credit monopolies "create", (print), Federal Reserve Notes that are then "lent" to the American government. This is a circular affair in that the government grants the FED power to create the money, which the FED then loans back to the government, charging interests. The government levies income taxes to pay the interest on the debt. It is interesting to note that the Federal Reserve Act and the sixteenth amendment which gave congress the power to collect income taxes, were both passed in 1913. The Federal Reserve Notes are not backed by anything of "intrinsic" value. (i.e., gold or silver).

On June 4, 1963, President, John Fitzgerald Kennedy signed a Presidential decree, Executive Order 11110, which stripped the Federal Reserve Banking System of its power to loan money to the United States Federal Government at interest. This decree meant that for every ounce of silver in the U.S. Treasury's vault, the U.S. government could introduce new money into circulation based on the silver bullion physically held therein. As a result, more than $4 trillion in United States Notes were brought into circulation in $2 and $5 denominations. $10 and $20 United States Notes were never circulated but were being printed by the Treasury Department when Kennedy was assassinated. Kennedy knew that if the silver backed United States Notes were widely circulated, they would have eliminated the demand for Federal Reserve Notes. By giving the U.S. Treasury the Constitutional authority to coin U.S. money once again, EO 11110 would thus prevent the national debt from rising due to "usury" that the American people are charged for "borrowing" (i.e., using) FRN's.

Kennedy knew that, if Congress coined and regulated money, as the Constitution states, the national debt would be reduced by not paying interest to the 12 credit monopolies. This in itself would have allowed the American people freedom to freely use all the money they have earned, enabling the economy to grow. Now, Executive Order 11110 is still in effect, even though no U.S. President has had the courage to follow it. As Americans, it is our duty to question the Federal Reserve System and the power that we have given it by electing presidents that lack the courage of John Fitzgerald Kennedy.

More on JFK's Executive Order 11110:
http://www.rense.com/general44/exec.htm

REPRINTED BY PERMISSION

FOUNDATION FOR TRUTH & LAW 2017

www.ingramcontent.com/pod-product-compliance
Lightning Source LLC
Chambersburg PA
CBHW060752260726
48660CB00002B/591